EPIGRAMMATA

EPIGRAMMATA

64 VERSE
MINIATURES

PETER DENMAN

For Ann Re.
John

Peter
Dec 2012

PHOTOGRAPHS AND PRINTS
KEVIN HONAN

ASTROLABE PRESS
DUBLIN
2012

COPYRIGHT 2012
by Peter Denman

ISBN 0-9548580-7-7

astrolabepress@gmail.com

For Siobhán
and Hugh and Feargus
with love

Acknowledgements

Some of these epigrams appeared previously in *Southword*. Number 53 was published, in a slightly different form, in *The Poet's Manual* collection (Sotto Voce Press, 1991). The opening line of 62 is taken from Michael Drayton's sonnet "Since there's no help"; that of 55 is adapted from Dylan Thomas's "Do Not Go Gentle Into That Good Night"; and that of 18 takes from Andrew Marvell's "To His Coy Mistress". 18 also steals from a poem by Carroll Daly.

Table of Contents

1

Between

. . . ourselves, two stools, the lines, and lovers,
The devil and the deep blue sea;
Waking and sleeping, one thing and another,
A rock and a hard place; you and me.

2

Two Women

Sharp-tongued Xantippe, always prone to rant,
Was scold and shrew and nag and termagant,
While Sappho's verses coming fast and loose
Show how her tongue was put to better use.

3

The File on Fixer

Health and safety rules were overlooked
When Fixer ran a nightclub, firedoors locked.
So Fixer chanced his arm, and thanks to him
Two hundred clubbers risked their life and limb.

4

Ariadne on Naxos

Poor thing – to think he would pick up the thread
With her, once he had left the beast for dead.

Theseus, having killed the Minotaur,
Prepared to cast his prize princess ashore.

The girl was pretty, and the sex was fine,
But he had learned how to wind up a line.

5

The Motorway

Across the median a six-mile tailback,
And we speed by on our reciprocal track.
They're stopped. We're not, so can't avoid a
Delighted glow of schadenfreude.

6

Health Note

Infections, cancers, strokes, - the list
Is long of possible diseases.
You cannot dodge them, so at least
Seek out some malady that pleases.

7

Charon

His budget airline flies across the Styx
With us, close-packed, seated in rows of six.
The flights are cheap; we get our money's worth;
He undertakes to bring us down to earth.

8

Gifts

The cold shoulder, or the common cold,
The steam off your piss, or an old-
Fashioned look; offence, a hoot, a brush-
Off, penny for your thoughts, the bum's rush.

9

The File on Fixer

Fresh from the tribunal, oozing unction,
Fixer turns up at his party's function.
For his party piece he sings a song
And, for that brief while, can do no wrong.

10

Sisyphus

I saw him lean against the rock and roll
It up the hill once more. Although that boulder,
Slipping and sliding, bruised his very soul
I think he loved its weight upon his shoulder.

11

FAQs

Here goes,
  What stays?
Who knows –
  Not days.

Who knows
  What's on?
Here goes –
  All gone.

12

Diana

The naked goddess glowered at the hunter
Who chanced within her bower to affront her.
"If this makes you feel horny, sir," she said,
"I'll satisfy you shortly on that head."

13

Day of Judgment

The marker reads the answers from his class,
Deciding who should fail and who should pass.
"An unexamined life is not worth living"
Says he, who has the grades within his giving.

14

Echo

From break of day to slow nightfall
He does not once return her call.
Condemned to hear herself, not him,
She dwindles to her eponym.

15

The File on Fixer

New leader needed; members have to choose,
So Fixer throws his hat into the ring,
Next adds his shirt and tie, his socks and shoes,
And then his trousers too, and everything.

His day job is to hoist the sky. At night he rests and lays it by. Then stars and galaxies are seen. And space. And more space in between...

28

16

Atlas

His day job is to hoist the sky.
At night he rests and lays it by.
Then stars and galaxies are seen.
And space. And more space in between.

17

Braille

His fingertips, working blind,
Print digital images on his mind.

18

Health Note

See how my eager self transpires
At every pore with instant fires.
Could this be love's own sweet cadenza?
Ah no, it's only influenza.

19

Apollo and Daphne

In hot pursuit, the god Apollo
Saw Daphne leaving and could not follow.

20

Health Note

This life is fast and fleet,
There is no turning back.
I don't mind the one-way-street,
But alas! the cul-de-sac.

21

The File on Fixer

Jetting acround the world, and on the make,
Fixer leaves a con-trail in his wake.

22

Penelope

Her suitors wait until the cloth is made,
Their patience, like the cloth, becoming frayed.

23

The Fates

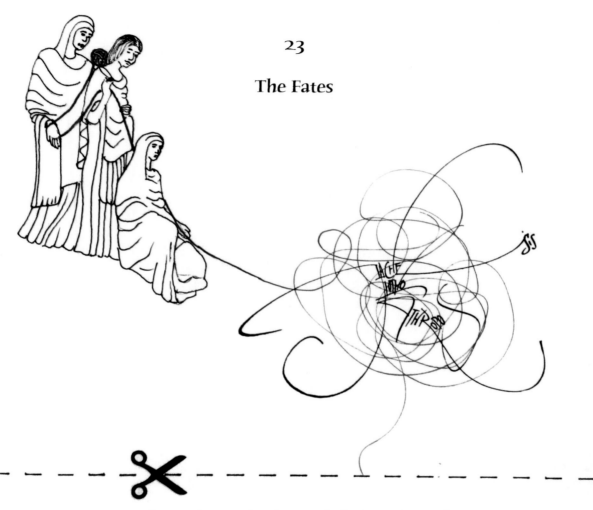

One spins, and spins me in her magic spell;
Another tempts me to pick up the thread;
There is a third, who toys with me as well,
And she is shaping up to cut me dead.

24

Object Lesson

Commitment had a schedule tightly planned
And bent each sinew to the task in hand,
While louche and laissez-faire Insouciance
Just let things roll and turn out well for once.

25

Féichín

The isle was crowded. Féichín offered mass
Beseeching God to cull the lower class.
God obliged. The plague raged far and wide.
The saint himself was one of those who died.

26

The Biographers

Prowling bookstacks, trawling archives,
Recording every fact that's known –
In writing up their subjects' lives
They end up writing off their own.

27

The File on Fixer

The council meets tonight to rezone lands
And Fixer watches as each member votes.
Minds change too when money changes hands
- He's not the only one who's taking notes.

28

Tantalus

For Tantalus, who could not sup nor feed,
Desire was inseparable from need -
And open-mouthed, while taking his last gasp,
He named a concept still beyond his grasp.

29

Health Note

I counted up each season
As round and round years sped;
But now I have more reason
To count them down instead.

30

Phaeton

We all admired his energy and dash
Until he lost control and had that crash.
The climate changed; he lay there in the sun
Surrounded by the wreck of what he'd done.

31

Social Occasion

I wonder why I came at all
To listen to their wretched chatter.
Their thoughts are trite; their talk is small;
They drop names with a dreadful clatter.

32

Philemon and Baucis

The grateful god gave what they had in mind;
Two trees above their graves grew intertwined.
So love endured. The trees stood deeply rooted
And year on year the meshing branches fruited.

33

The File on Fixer

Fixer has some money he must launder
And hide within the shadow of a doubt.
He builds a plush hotel and leisure centre
-- It gives him somewhere he can lie about.

34

Danae

Danae, locked inside her tower,
Was taken by the golden shower.
Jove gave, to get into her bed,
A rain-check for her maidenhead.

35

Moral Index

The virtues, if we believe St Paul,
Are Faith, and Hope, and Charity;
This last performs the best of all -
Its stock trades over parity.

36

Biography

With all his hopes of Maud gone
(And of her daughter, young Iseult)
Yeats decided to move on
To George, who offered the occult.
And, whether she was true or fraud,
His book, *A Vision,* did result.
Poems were all he got from Maud
(And even less from young Iseult).

37

Medusa

Just watch out when she gives you head:
She'll make you hard; she'll leave you dead.

38

Last Word

Enough is enough. It's a zero sum
Everything reaches equilibrium,
With loose ends tucked in their proper places
Let's call a halt. Full stop. Stasis.

39

The File on Fixer

Avarice, Venality, Deceit –
Deals are done whenever these three meet.
Fixer joins them, makes a fourth,
Selling himself for all that he is worth.

40

Aegeus

He yearned to know his son was coming back
And watched upon the cliff top all day long.
He saw the ship, and saw the sails were black,
Then jumped to a conclusion which was wrong.

41

Astrolabe

A girl who studies with a tutor
Takes other lessons from her suitor.
Failure to distinguish these
Undid my mother, Heloise.

42

Helen

Word of mouth, and rumour, and repute,
Would have us believe that Helen was a beaut;
But, with Hector dead and Troy destroyed, she shall
Be ever thought of as the femme fatale.

43

Two Men

Devil-May-Care glows with panache,
His gestures broad, his manner brash.
God-Help-Us fades away as usual
To hide his light beneath a bushel.
And this is how the world is made
A half in sun and half in shade.

44

Cerberus

I raged against the dying of the light.
As night fell roughly all I saw was red.
And then at last my dark-adapted sight
Made out the black dog growling up ahead.

45

The File on Fixer

Fraud or scam, a stroke, or handy nixer,
He's in for what's in it for Fixer.

46

The Fun of the Fair

We're coins on the fairground slider
Pushed ever nearer the edge.
If only the platform were wider
We might not fall off the ledge.

But they keep on adding a coin
As the platform moves to and fro,
And whenever a couple more join
One of us has to slip off and go.

For such is is the balance of power;
We can't get the platform to stop.
We know not the day nor the hour
That the penny will finally drop.

47

Ferns

"Suffer little children . . ." The priest commands.
And then the boys are *putti* in his hands.

48

Orpheus

"DON'T LOOK ROUND"
WAS THE DECREE,
BUT LOOK HE MUST
AND SENT EURIDICE
HURTLING BACK TO
HELL
WAS IT LOVE THAT
TURNED HIS HEAD
OR LACK OF TRUST?
THE QUESTION ROSE
EVEN AS SHE FELL.

49

Autograph Tree

Poets and playwrights – all and each
Inscribed, while visiting Coole Park,
Initials on the copper beech.

These days, to protect the bark
Its trunk is caged and out of reach.
No modern writer makes a mark.

50

Ixion

Ixion on his wheel has found
Sufficient pain to go around;
By watching him revolve we learn
That each man suffers in his turn.

51

The File on Fixer

Circles he moves in keep him in the loop
And willing to jump through any hoop.
Fixer works the room, tries out his charm,
And smiles and smiles with polished smarm.

52

Narcissus

Despondent by his pond, grown thin
And old, he ponders which to pour:
Oil on the troubled waters, or
Botox in his wrinkled skin.

53

Protestant Cemetery, Caen

Beau Brummel's last sartorial grace
Attends him in this final place.
Deep in his changing-room he lies
Trying on the earth for size.

54

Daedalus

Great paintings show, and many verses tell
How Icarus flew too high, and burned, and fell;
But Daedalus merits only this poor rhyme:
He stayed on course, and landed safe, on time.

55

Epitaph

Stick-in-the-Mud, who lately died,
Was cautiousness personified.
We bury him in what may prove
His very first ground-breaking move.

56

Leda

Bold Jove, intent to try it on
With Leda, morphed into a swan;
He knew it took some neck to mount her
On what was just their first encounter.

57

Protestant Cemetery, Rome

His ashes placed at Shelley's feet
Greg Corso rests here now, dead beat.

58

The File on Fixer

Some people cast their bread upon the waters
And wonder what they'll get.
But Fixer, never one for taking chances,
Prefers to cast a net.

59

Terminal

Debouched into Arrivals, I
Scan the placards held on high.
I flew here a complete unknown
And plan to travel on alone,
Yet - half expectant, half afraid -
Still check in case my name's displayed.

60

Rebus

E is a bit of energy to start;
For closure find a forceful rhyme to slam;
Add in some beastly matter at its heart,
And that's the making of an e-pig-ram.

61

Thus Spake

From Apollo we can trace
Beauty, order, line and grace.
Where there's riot, where there's wrack
- That is Dionysiac.
These ideas are Friedrich Nietzsche's.
Frenzy's good (or so he preaches)

62

Last Things Last

Shake hands for ever, cancel all our vows
And leave our balance quite unreconciled:
A sudden dispensation that allows
Us go our separate ways, and love run wild.

The rule of hurt is coming hard and fast,
Blown in the wind are straws at which we clutch;
And in the end we gather last things last:
Our hands are shaking. It's the final touch.

63

The File on Fixer

Fixer, who had his price for which he'd sell,
Now stares out through the bar-code of a cell.

64

Aetatis Suae

Eight times eight, or four by four by four;
I've lived those times, and would not mind some more.

Notes

The "Fixer" figure is a composite from Ireland of the recent past.

The figures from classical myth and history whose stories are drawn upon are, I hope, well known or easily sourced, but it may be useful to gloss the following:

24 - this legend attaches to Saint Féichín who had a monastery in the beautiful valley of Fore, Co. Westmeath, in the 7th century;

41 - Heloise fell in love with her tutor Abelard, and things turned out badly for them. Astrolabe was their son;

47 - the Ferns Report in 2005 revealed the extent of clerical sex abuse of children in that diocese;

50 - Xantippe was the wife of Socrates and a proverbial scold;

53 - Beau Brummel is buried in Caen, Normandy, the town in which he spent his unhappy last years of exile and poverty;

56 - Gregory Corso's ashes were interred, by special dispensation, at a spot next to Shelley's grave in Rome; the reference to Shelley's feet is poetic licence, as in his case also it is his ashes that are buried there.